The Joy Nursery Rhymes

Arranged by Cyril Ornadel.

Yorktown Music Press / Music Sales Limited
London / New York / Paris / Sydney / Copenhagen / Madrid

Exclusive Distributors:
Music Sales Limited
8/9 Frith Street, London W1V 5TZ, England.
Music Sales Pty Limited
120 Rothschild Avenue, Rosebery, NSW 2018, Australia.
Music Sales Corporation
257 Park Avenue South, New York, NY 10010, United States of America.

This book © Copyright 1994 by Yorktown Music Press / Music Sales Limited
Order No. AM91357
ISBN 0-7119-3616-1

Compiled by Peter Evans.
Music edited by Cyril Ornadel.
Music processed by Ternary Graphics.

Music Sales' complete catalogue describes thousands of titles and is available in
full colour sections by subject, direct from Music Sales Limited.
Please state your areas of interest and send a cheque/postal order for £1.50 for postage to:
Music Sales Limited, Newmarket Road, Bury St. Edmunds, Suffolk IP33 3YB.

Your Guarantee of Quality:
As publishers, we strive to produce every book to the highest commercial standards.
The music has been freshly engraved and the book has been carefully designed to minimise
awkward page turns and to make playing from it a real pleasure.
Particular care has been given to specifying acid-free, neutral-sized paper made from
pulps which have not been elemental chlorine bleached.
This pulp is from farmed sustainable forests and was produced with special regard for the environment.
Throughout, the printing and binding have been planned to ensure a sturdy,
attractive publication which should give years of enjoyment.
If your copy fails to meet our high standards, please inform us and we will gladly replace it.

Printed in the United Kingdom by
J.B. Offset Printers (Marks Tey) Limited, Marks Tey, Essex.

Baa Baa Black Sheep

Traditional

Baa   Baa   Black   Sheep   have   you   a - ny   wool?

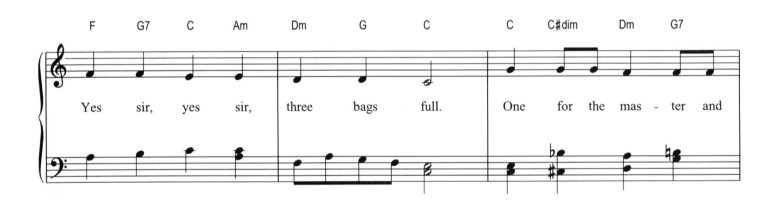

Yes   sir,   yes   sir,   three   bags   full.   One   for   the   mas - ter   and

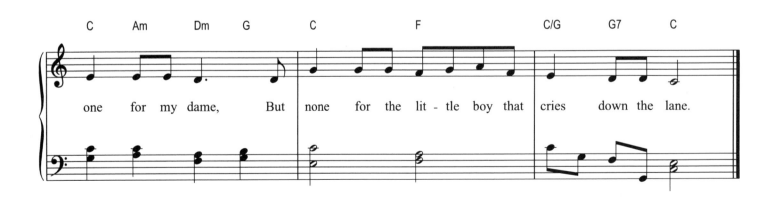

one   for   my   dame,   But   none   for   the   lit - tle   boy   that   cries   down   the   lane.

Bobby Shaftoe

Traditional

Diddle, Diddle Dumpling,
My Son John

Traditional

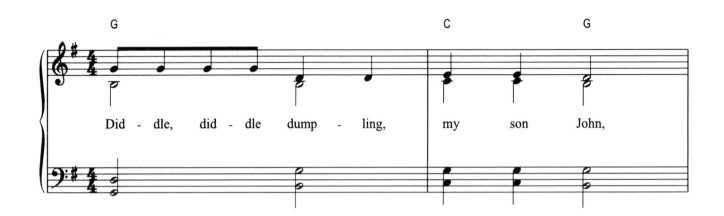

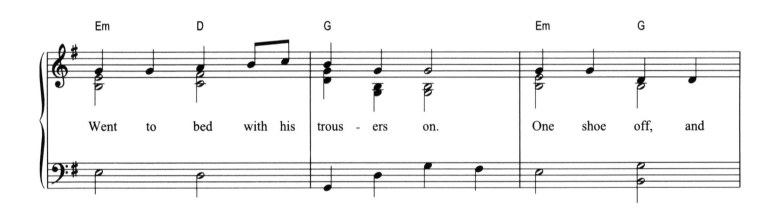

Ding Dong Bell

Traditional

Ding dong bell! Pus - sy's in the well.

Who put her in? Lit - tle Tom - my Green. Who pulled her out?

Lit - tle Tom - my Stout. What a naugh - ty boy was that to drown poor pus - sy cat, who

ne'er did an - y harm, but killed ___ all the mice in his fa - ther's barn.

Eensy Weensy Spider

Traditional

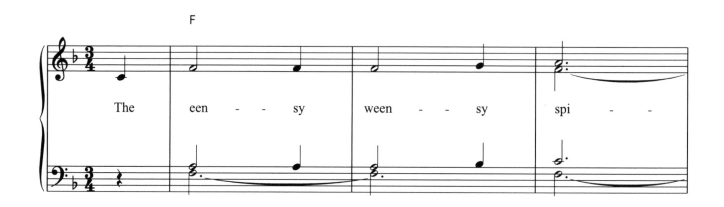

The een - - sy ween - - sy spi - -

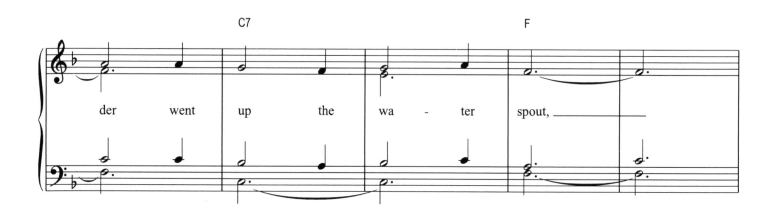

der went up the wa - ter spout, _____

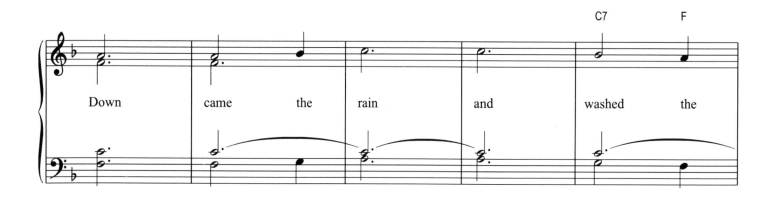

Down came the rain and washed the

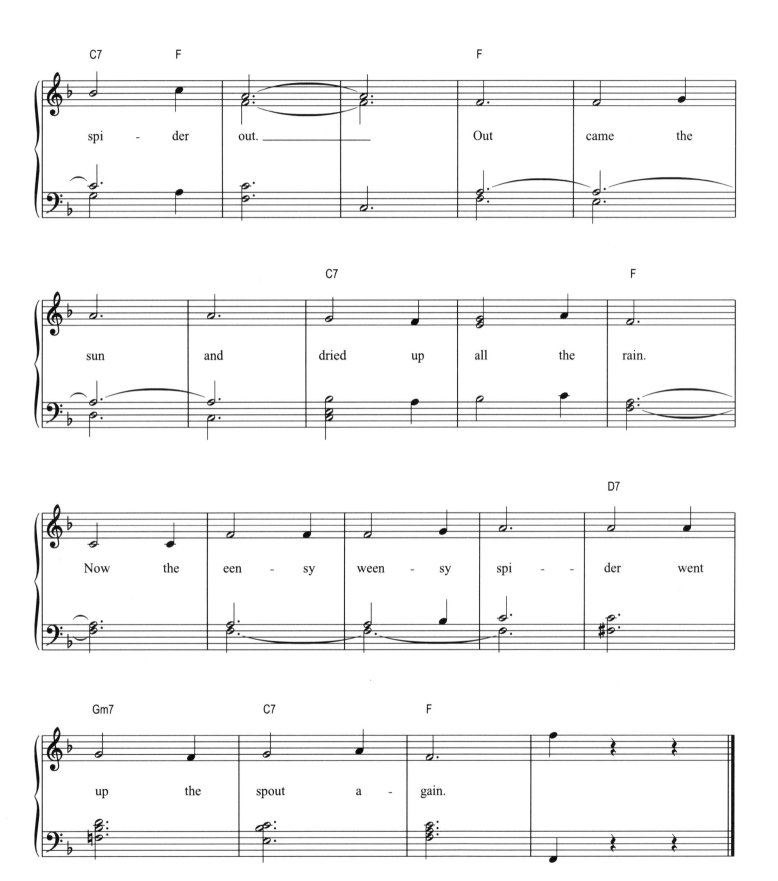

Frère Jacques

Traditional

Frè – re Jac – ques, Frè – re Jac – ques,

Dor – mez vous? Dor – mez vous? Son – nez les ma – ti – nes,

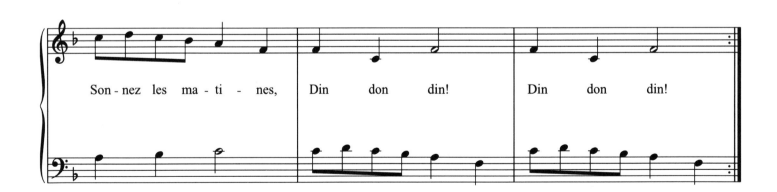

Son – nez les ma – ti – nes, Din don din! Din don din!

Georgie Porgie

Traditional

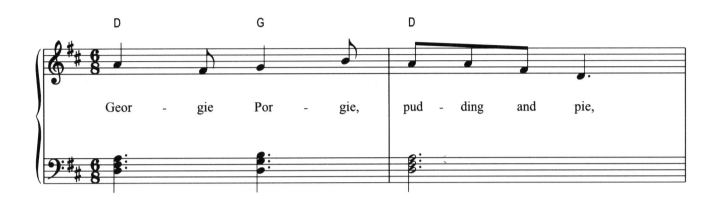

Geor - gie Por - gie, pud - ding and pie,

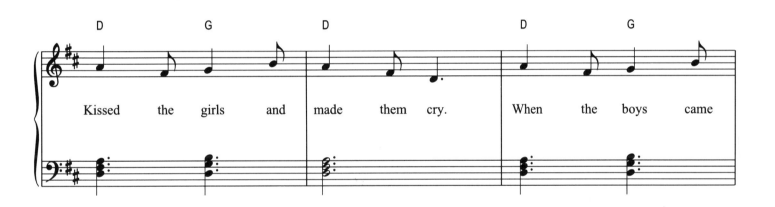

Kissed the girls and made them cry. When the boys came

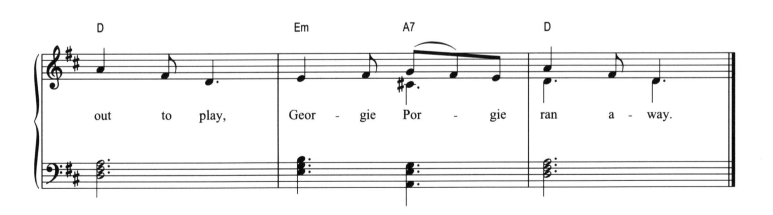

out to play, Geor - gie Por - gie ran a - way.

Girls And Boys Come Out To Play

Traditional

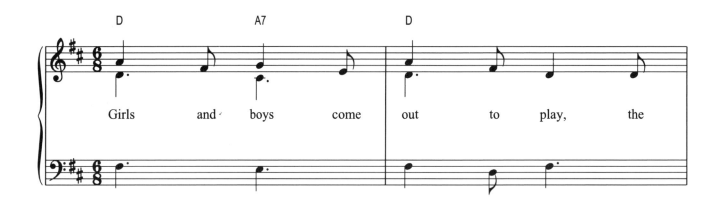

Girls and boys come out to play, the

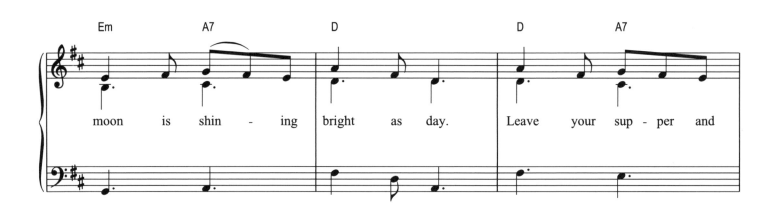

moon is shin - ing bright as day. Leave your sup - per and

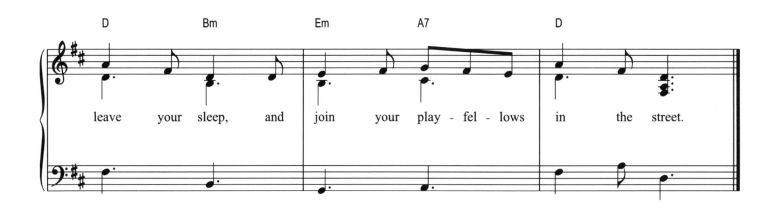

leave your sleep, and join your play - fel - lows in the street.

The Grand Old Duke Of York

Traditional

13

Here We Go Round The Mulberry Bush

Traditional

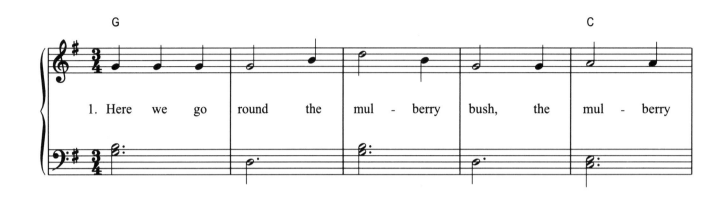

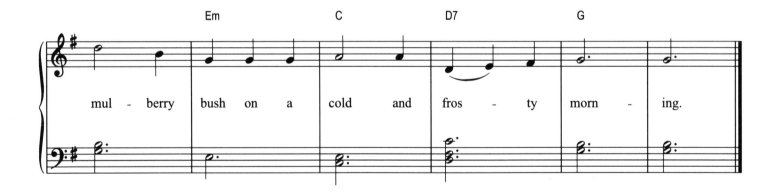

2. This is the way we wash our hands…
3. This is the way we wash our clothes…
4. This is the way we dry our clothes…
5. This is the way we iron our clothes…
6. This is the way we sweep the floor…
7. This is the way we brush our hair…
8. This is the way we go to school…
9. This is the way we come back from school…

Hey Diddle Diddle

Traditional

Hickory Dickory Dock

Traditional

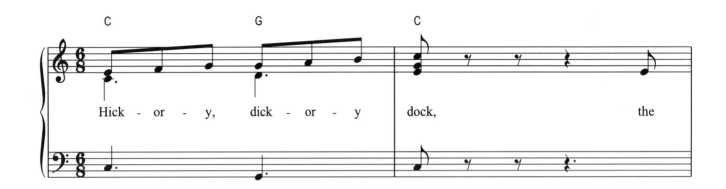

Hick - or - y, dick - or - y dock, the

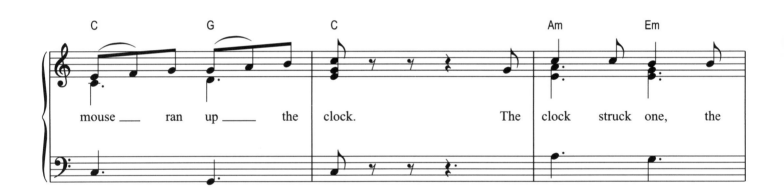

mouse ___ ran up ___ the clock. The clock struck one, the

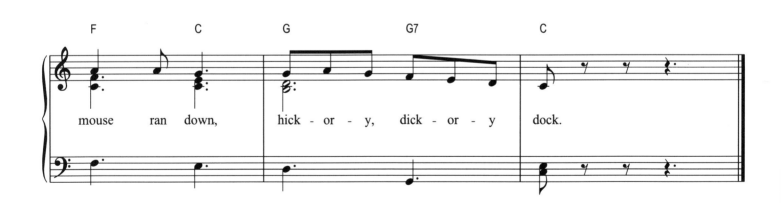

mouse ran down, hick - or - y, dick - or - y dock.

Humpty Dumpty

Traditional

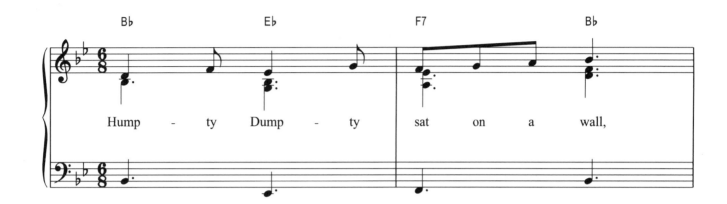

Hump - ty Dump - ty sat on a wall,

Hump - ty Dump - ty had a great fall. All the King's hors - es and

all the King's men Could - n't put Hump - ty to - geth - er a - gain.

I Had A Little Nut Tree

Traditional

2. I had a little nut tree
    Nothing would it bear
    But a silver nutmeg and a golden pear.
    I skipped over water,
    I danced over sea,
    And all the birds in the air
    Couldn't catch me.

I Saw Three Ships

Traditional

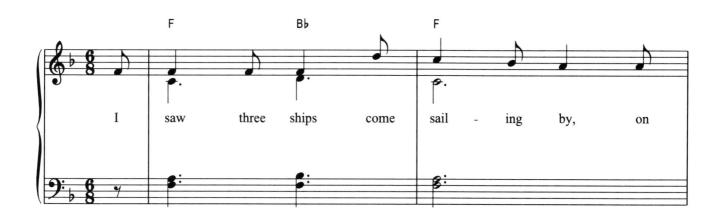

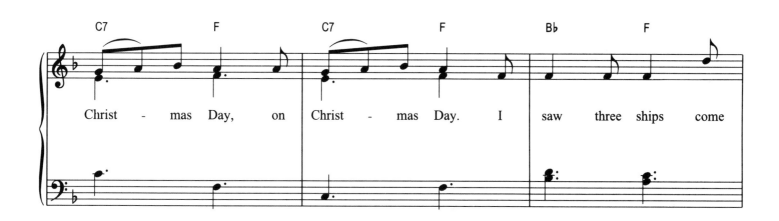

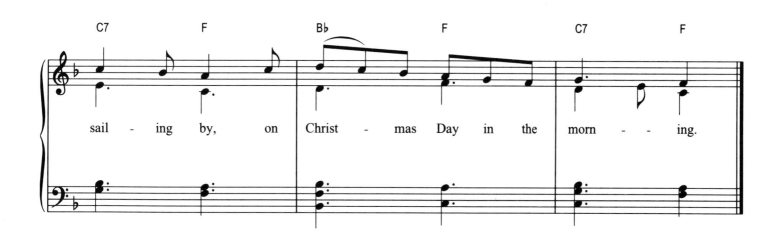

Jack And Jill

Traditional

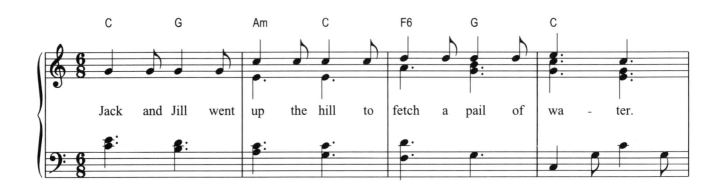

Jack and Jill went up the hill to fetch a pail of wa - ter.

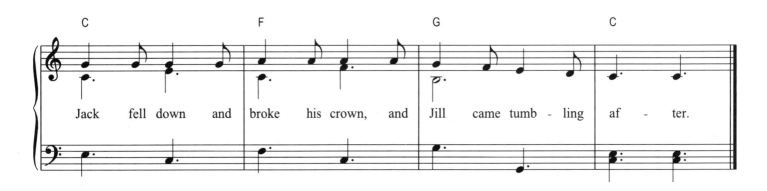

Jack fell down and broke his crown, and Jill came tumb - ling af - ter.

Ladybird, Ladybird

Traditional

La - dy - bird, la - dy - bird, fly a - way home, your house is on fire and your chil-dren all gone.

Lavender's Blue

Traditional

2. Call up your men, dilly dilly,
    Set them to work.
    Some to the plough, dilly dilly,
    Some to the cart.

3. Some to make hay, dilly, dilly,
    Some to cut corn.
    Whilst you and I, dilly, dilly,
    Keep ourselves warm.

4. Roses are red, dilly, dilly,
    Violets are blue.
    If you love me, dilly, dilly,
    I will love you.

5. Let the birds sing, dilly, dilly,
    And the lambs play.
    We shall be safe, dilly, dilly,
    Out of harm's way.

Little Bo-Peep

Traditional

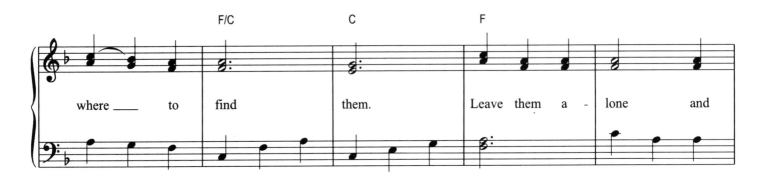

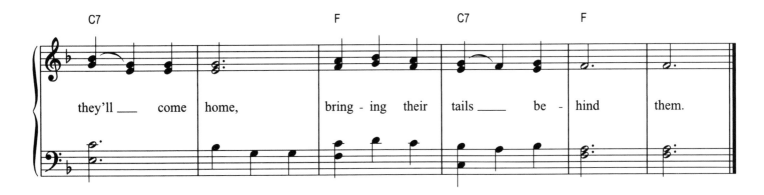

2. Little Bo-Peep fell fast asleep
    And dreamed she heard them bleating.
    But when she awoke, she found it a joke,
    For they were still a-fleeting.

3. Then up she took, her little crook,
    Determined for to find them.
    She found them indeed, but it made her heart bleed,
    For they'd left their tails behind them.

Little Boy Blue

Traditional

© Copyright 1994 Dorsey Brothers Music Limited, 8/9 Frith Street, London W1.

Little Jack Horner

Traditional

Little Miss Muffet

Traditional

London Bridge Is Falling Down

Traditional

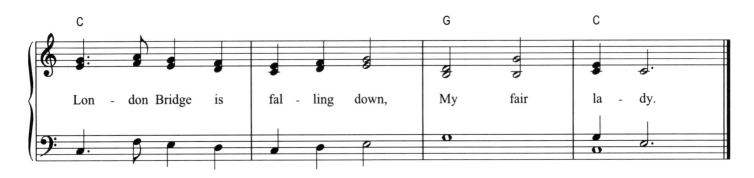

2. Build it up with iron bars…
3. Iron bars will bend and break…
4. Build it up with pins and needles…
5. Pins and needles rust and bend…
6. Build it up with penny loaves…
7. Penny loaves will tumble down…
8. Build it up with gold and silver…
9. Gold and silver I've not got…
10. Here's a prisoner I have got…
11. What's the prisoner done to you?…
12. Stole my watch and broke my chain…
13. What'll you take to set him free?…
14. One hundred pounds will set him free…
15. One hundred pounds we have not got…
16. Then off to prison he must go…

Mary Had A Little Lamb

Traditional

2.   And everywhere that Mary went,
Mary went, Mary went,
Everywhere that Mary went
The lamb was sure to go.

3.   It followed her to school one day,
School one day, school one day,
Followed her to school one day,
That was against the rule.

4.   It made the children laugh and play,
Laugh and play, laugh and play,
Made the children laugh and play
To see the lamb at school.

Mary, Mary, Quite Contrary

Traditional

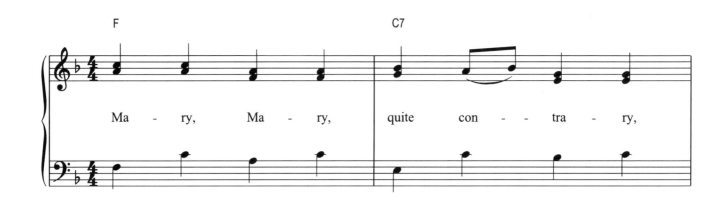

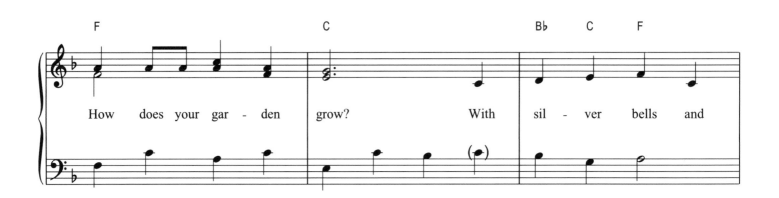

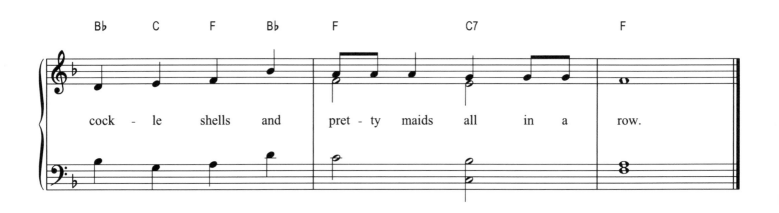

Oh, Dear! What Can The Matter Be?

Traditional

Oh Where, Oh Where Has My Little Dog Gone?

Traditional

Old King Cole

Traditional

Old MacDonald

Traditional

* pigs   ** oink-oink
* ducks   ** quack-quack
* cows   ** moo-moo

Oranges And Lemons

Traditional

Old Mother Hubbard

Traditional

Verses

3.   She went to the undertaker's
To buy him a coffin:
But when she came back
The poor dog was laughing.

4.   She took a clean dish
To get him some tripe:
But when she got back
He was smoking a pipe.

5.   She went to the fishmonger's
To buy him some fish:
But when she came back
He was licking the dish.

6.   She went to the tavern
For white wine and red:
But when she got back
The dog stood on his head.

7.   She went to the fruiterer's
To buy him some fruit:
But when she came back
He was playing the flute.

8.   She went to the tailor's
To buy him a coat:
But when she came back
He was riding a goat.

9.   She went to the hatter's
To buy him a hat
But when she came back
He was feeding the cat.

10.   She went to the barber's
To buy him a wig:
But when she came back
He was dancing a jig.

11.   She went to the cobbler's
To buy him some shoes:
But when she came back
He was reading the news.

12.   She went to the seamstress
To buy him some linen:
But when she came back
The dog was a-spinning.

13.   She went to the hosier's
To buy him some hose:
But when she came back
He was dressed in his clothes.

14.   The Dame made a curtsey,
The dog made a bow;
The Dame said, your servant,
The dog said, "Bow-wow".

Pat-A-Cake, Pat-A-Cake, Baker's Man

Traditional

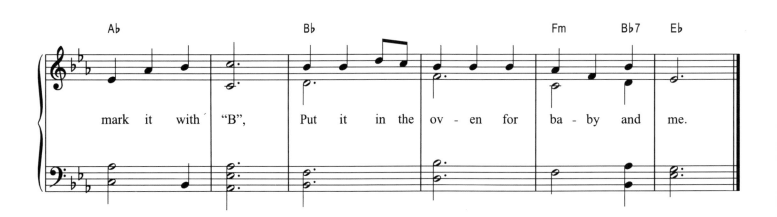

Pease Porridge Hot

Traditional

Pease por-ridge hot, Pease por-ridge cold, Pease por-ridge in the pot nine days old.

Pop Goes The Weasel

Traditional

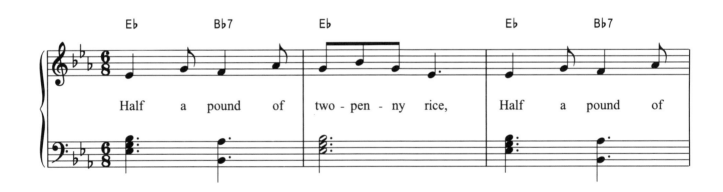

Half a pound of two-pen - ny rice, Half a pound of

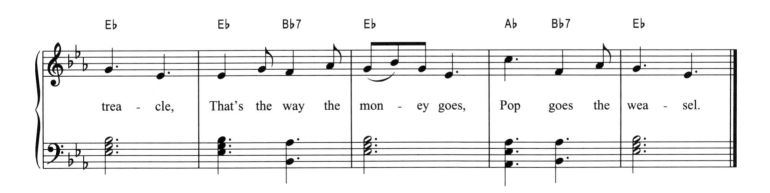

trea - cle, That's the way the mon - ey goes, Pop goes the wea - sel.

Polly Put The Kettle On

Traditional

Pussy Cat, Pussy Cat

Traditional

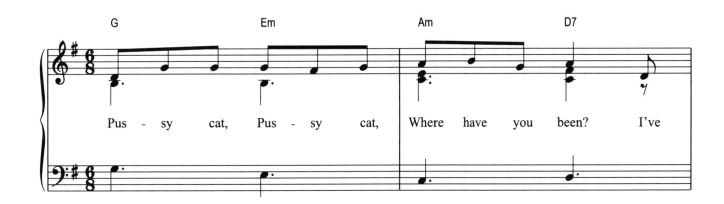

Pus - sy cat, Pus - sy cat, Where have you been? I've

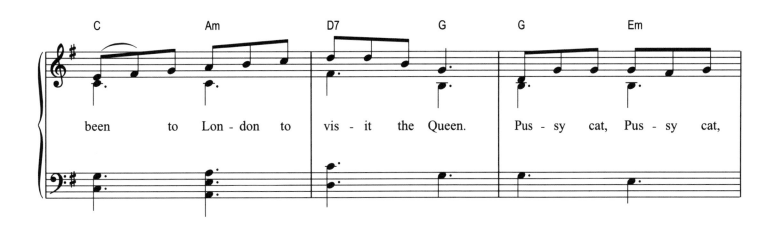

been to Lon - don to vis - it the Queen. Pus - sy cat, Pus - sy cat,

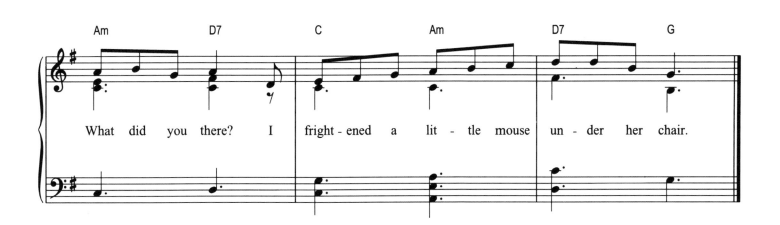

What did you there? I fright - ened a lit - tle mouse un - der her chair.

Ring-A-Ring O' Roses

Traditional

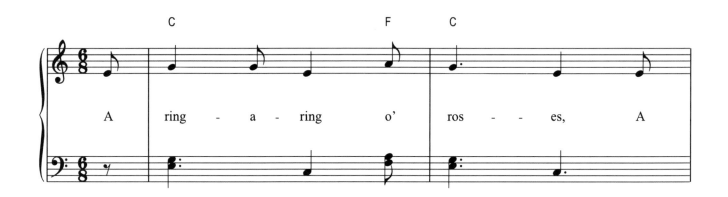

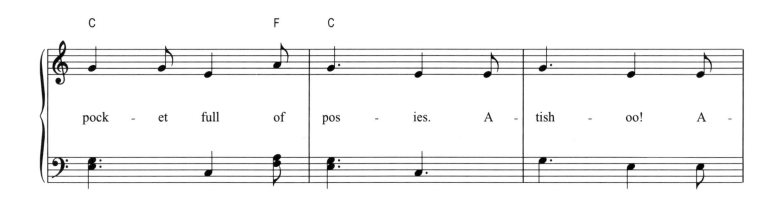

Rock-A-Bye Baby

Traditional

Row, Row, Row Your Boat

Traditional

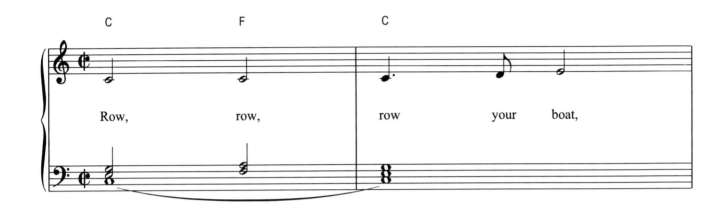

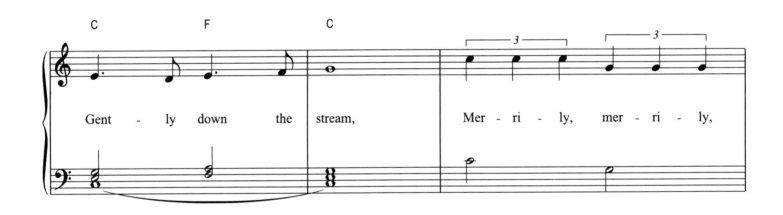

Simple Simon

Traditional

Sim - ple Sim - on met a pie - man

go - ing to the fair, _____ Said Sim - ple Sim - on

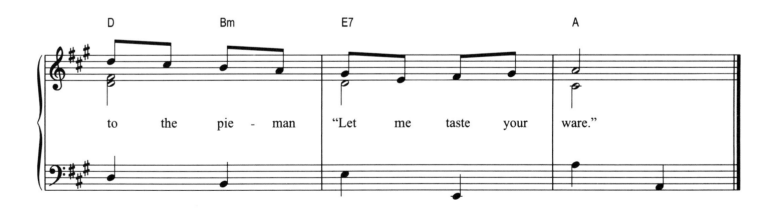

to the pie - man "Let me taste your ware."

Sing A Song Of Sixpence

Traditional

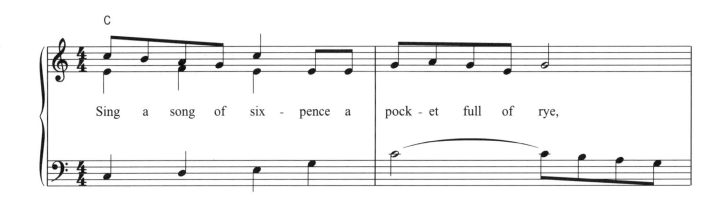

Skip To My Lou

Traditional

Lou,   Lou,   Skip to my Lou,   Lou,   Lou,   Skip to my Lou,

Lou,   Lou,   Skip to my Lou,   Skip to my Lou, my   dar - ling.

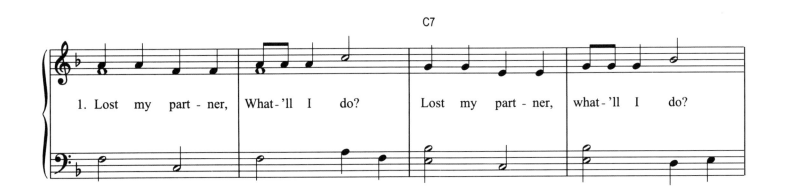

1. Lost my part - ner,   What - 'll I   do?   Lost my part - ner,   what - 'll I   do?

Lost my part - ner, What-'ll I do? Skip to my Lou, my dar - ling.

Lou, Lou, Skip to my Lou. Lou, Lou, Skip to my Lou,

Lou, Lou, Skip to my Lou, Skip to my Lou my dar - ling.

2. I'll find another one, prettier than you…
3. Little red wagon, painted blue…
4. Can't get a red bird, a blue bird'll do…
5. Cows in the meadow, moo, moo, moo…
6. Flies in the meadow, shoo, shoo, shoo…

There's A Hole In My Bucket

Traditional

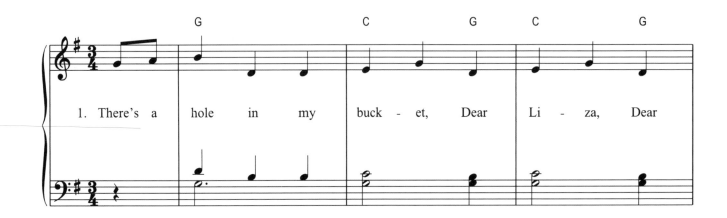

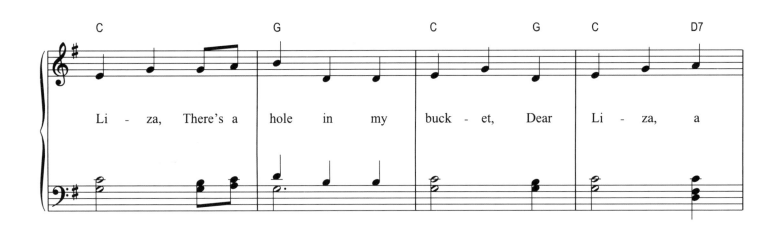

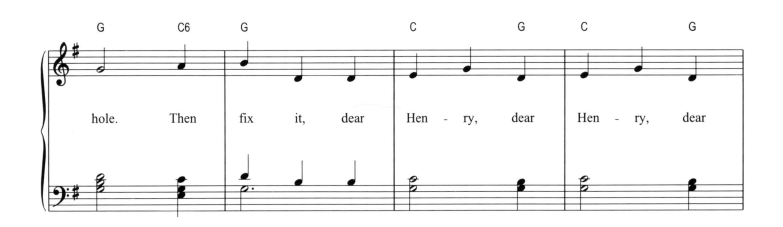

2.   With what shall I fix it?
       Dear Liza, dear Liza,
       With what shall I fix it?
       Dear Liza, with what?

Three Blind Mice

Traditional

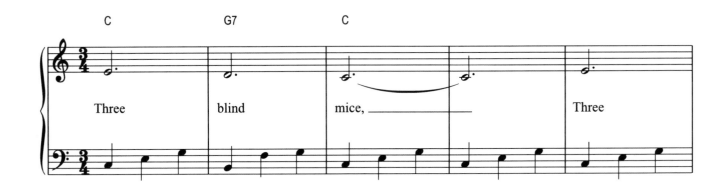

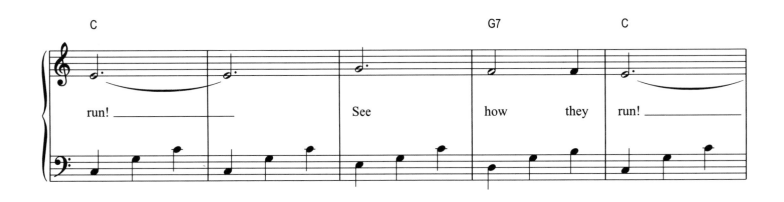

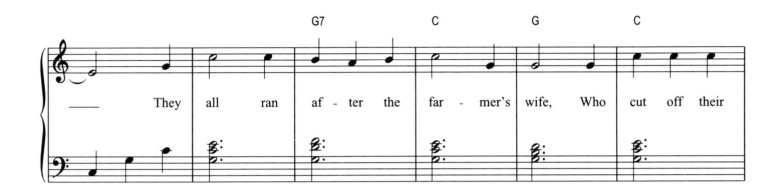

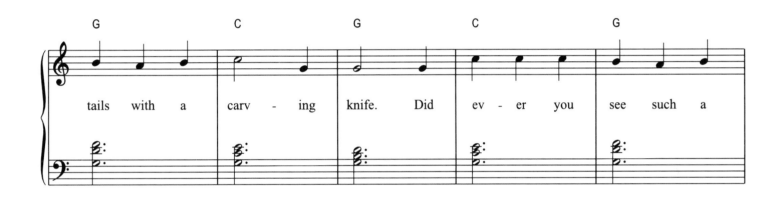

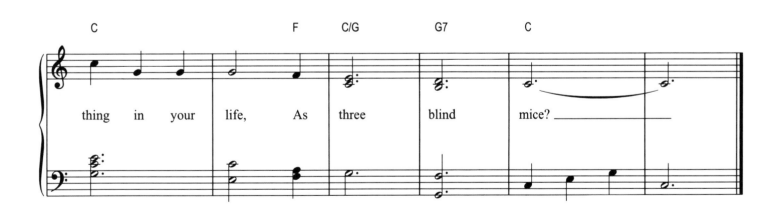

The Muffin Man

Traditional

Tom, Tom, The Piper's Son

Traditional

Twinkle, Twinkle, Little Star

Traditional

Wee Willie Winkie

Traditional

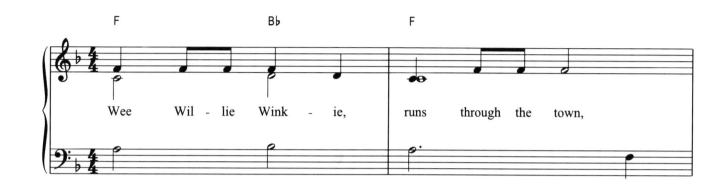

Wee Wil - lie Wink - ie, runs through the town,

Up - stairs and down - stairs in his night - gown. Rap - ping at the win - dow,

Cry - ing through the lock, Are the child - ren all in bed, For now it's eight o'clock?

Yankee Doodle

Traditional

5/94 (17981)